FOREST BOOKS

PATTERNS

FEDERICO MAYOR was born in Barcelona, Spain in 1934. In 1956 he graduated in Pharmacy with a special award (Premio extraordinario), from Complutense University, Madrid. He completed his doctorate with further awards and five years later became Professor of Biochemistry at the University of Granada. A distinguished career in this field led to his appointment as Under-Secretary for the Spanish Ministry of Education and Science in 1974. A year later he became Chairman of the Advisory Committe for Scientific and Technical Research. It was soon after this, as a member of the Advisory Committee on the European Center for Higher Education (CEPES) of UNESCO in Romania, that his life with UNESCO began. He worked in Moscow and in Paris. His interests were also in Special Education and Parliament, and by 1977 he was advisor to the Spanish Prime Minister. However he managed to combine his interests. In 1978 he was appointed Deputy Director-General of UNESCO and in 1987 Director-General. In the same year he also become a member of the European Parliament.

He has received many academic decorations and honours from all over the world.

Patterns

FEDERICO MAYOR

translated by
ROSEMARY WILTSHIRE

and introduced by
EDOUARD J. MAUNICK

FOREST
BOOKS
London & Boston

PUBLISHED BY
FOREST BOOKS

20 Forest View, Chingford, London E4 7AY, UK
PO BOX 312, Lincoln Centre, MA 01773, USA

FIRST PUBLISHED
1994 3/2/94

Typeset in Great Britain by Fleetlines Typesetters, Southend-on-Sea
Printed in Great Britain by BPCC Wheatons Ltd, Exeter

Original Poems © Federico Mayor
Translations © Rosemary Wiltshire
Introduction © Edouard J. Maunick
Cover design © Ian Evans

Library of Congress Catalogue Card No. 93-74145

A CIP catalogue record for this book is available from the
British Library

ISBN 1-85610-034-0

ACKNOWLEDGEMENTS
Poems on pages, 27, 33, 34 and 42 have been published by Angel
Caffarena, Libreria Anticuaria El Guadalhorce, Malaga, 1988 under the
title En transito.
Poems on pages 52 and 67 have appeared in the Revue des deux
Mondes, December, 1989.
The poem on page 53 was published in the periodical O Comercio do
Porto on 9.7.89 in the supplement Cultura e Arte.
The poem on page 71, was published in The Unesco Courier in June
1990

Reading *Patterns*

You name the place, he has been there. Not alone because it is his duty to travel. To go and meet the people where they are, in the midst of their everyday life. To deliver speeches and to listen. He has been there also because the poet is born to be on the road. Again and again. From Yamoussoukro to the Asturias, from Algiers to Tokyo, Federico Mayor is not just a high ranking international official on his way to and from a mission however useful and serious it may be. This is the duty he has chosen to fulfil and that must be performed. But there is that other part he plays and for which he has been chosen. No one is ever able to say by whom. And how. And why. Poetry being solely responsible, at all levels, and who would dare submit poetry to the question. From Munich to Maputo, from Chinguitti to Beijing, he makes no effort to interrupt what he has discovered to be the voice of the universe. Why should he?

The words are there, sappy and ready to flow in order to name those who must not live and die anonymous. Federico Mayor, the poet, knows how to fill silence and emptiness. He seems to have learned everything from nature. Though being a scientist, he accepts and yields to emotion, the key to wonder. The great privilege has been mine to have read *Patterns* in the original Spanish, to have worked on the French translation and to simply react here to the English version, as a poet testifying in favour of another poet he wishes both the individual and the crowd to listen and to hear. The wonder opens with the word in whatever language it is being written. And concerning the word, Federico Mayor's poetry reminds me of what Roger Caillois wrote with so much appropriateness: *"Every word is a trap, a seed, a ferment, a starting point for the soul and not a finishing line for intelligence. . ."* (Art poétique, 1958).

The sea is everywhere in Mayor's poems, even when he keeps from naming it. The oppressing sea. The disturbing sea. But, most of all, the sea around Salobrena in whose waves are the birth, the death and the resurrection of the poem, when, as in *Patterns*, it springs from 'the infinite depths of each one of us/where the visible is forged/to make fertile the parched crust'. I was born in an island in the far off Indian Ocean. "Claveles" (carnation) was the first Spanish word I learnt to pronounce; and the sea is the one and only season of my poetry. While going through *Patterns*, it often seems to me that Federico Mayor has been cruising all along my coral reefs and blue lagoon, and that Salobrena is a Catalan mermaid with a fair Creole accent. I feel sometimes so close to Mayor's poetry that I wish I had written this line of his, the last I quote: 'But I am going. . ./and the sea is going with me!'

Edouard J. Maunick Paris 1993

Patterns is a selection
of poems, of feelings and
words I have written while
in different parts of the
world, which I wish to share
with those who believe it is
still possible to forge a
common future more in harmony
with human dignity. And,
especially, with those who
believe the opposite.

Las cosas que veo son
mías y de las que no veo
poseo justo la mitad.
Proverbio árabe.

Cuando me pidan
cuál es mi estirpe
diré que soy linaje
del universo entero,
de este cauce inagotable,
de esta urdimbre
de unidades
arracimadas,
de este tejido mestizo
grandioso, fecundo
y pasajero.

Hacia la sombra fluyo.
¿O hacia la plenitud?
Mi libertad está aquí:
este es el único consuelo.

Munich, Schloss Rinberg,
8/10/85

Things I see are mine
and I own 50% of
what I do not see.
Arab proverb.

When they ask me
what is my background
I shall say I come from
the whole universe,
from this unceasing flow,
from this weft
of clustered
threads,
from this weave of mixtures
great, fertile
and passing.

I flow towards darkness.
Or towards wholeness?
My freedom is here:
this is the one consolation.

Munich, Schloss Reinberg,
8/10/85

'L'horaire des trains
dépasse les livres sacrés'
Boris Pasternak

Why come back tomorrow,
why rise early
and run
the same rounds,
and see, again,
the rich
short-sighted
and the poor
long-sighted?
Why hurry?
To what,
for what,
to arrive on time?
Time-tables
have suppressed
life and rhythm.
Books lie unopened.
And yet,
there, is hidden
the word we yearn for.

For Edouard Maunick
Paris, 10/12/90

'No puedes esperar hasta que Dios llegue a t
y te diga: yo soy . . .'
Raine María Rilke
(in "Adviento")

To meet You
each night
without finding You!
That is
the highest possibility
You have given us:
to live freely
roaming questioning
and certainties
until one day, at last,
we know.
Today, Your footsteps alone.

December 90

Light
beats down
on my aching eyes.
Night
moves away
from the dark life
of these brothers of ours
unnoticed,
abandoned to their fate.

No bed,
nor roof,
only rags
around their thin
bodies. . .

The castle
reflecting the splendour
– of some –
of times past
brings its strict
reference to bear. . .
(Today we build rockets,
war planes. . .)
Reality is clear:
abandoned to their fate!
Neither their life
nor their death
matters to us.

Gondar, in a place called 'Goha'
Ethiopia, 5/1/89

The river stills heavy
and troubled.
My heart
echoes
    each beat.

I cannot leave you here
in this mist
for ever,
in this earth
beneath the wretched
tree.

We started out together
and together we will continue
upstream

You will be
a shining teardrop
along my way.

For Marie-Annic Martin-Sané
St Jean s/Mayenne, 8/1/88

I am so wretched,
sea,
I am so poor,
and you with your wealth
of depth,
of colour
and horizons.

Powerful,
vast sea!

And yet
you cannot withstand my strength:
I look at you,
know you,
love you.

Salobreña, Summer 1986.

I dream
of seeing thousands of teachers
file by . . .

Our wars
are other wars:
to help
those broken
by drugs
or wine,
the disabled,
the child
the lonely,
those wounded
by bullets,
by routine
or by oblivion,
the old. . .

Other soldiers
I should like to see
strong, invincible,
with other weapons
and other goals. . .

(While the crowds
pass by
millions of illiterate people
live and die).

For Sujata & Ananda Guruge
Paris, 14/7/80.

Enjoy every minute
of your life
as if you were
just on the brink
of losing it,
as if you would have
trembled in the face of the great
lesson of courage
of those who drain
knowlingly
the last drops
of their days,
or resist
wretchedness,
suffering,
ignorance.

It is here
wherein we can find
the essence of things,
the spring of happiness
and of hope,
and not in the meetings
where the rich
discuss the problems of the poor,
or men
the situation of women,
or adults
the behaviour of youth. . .

Enjoy every minute.
Each minute
longer and deeper
as you move toward
sunset. . .

How wonderful to live
and see
and laugh
and shout
in the face of the ever nearing
horizon
of silence
and emptiness.

Everything will go on
as before.
And there,
what is it?
Where?

July 1982

Your child-eyes
have already seen
the horror
of war,
of violence,
of hunger. . .

Your eyes have seen
the wound
and the blood,
hatred,
and
harshness.

Your child-eyes
have seen only
coldness
and flashes of anger. . .

Live, child of Beirut,
so that one day
you may see the greatness
of the light
sheltering
beneath the human skin.

For any child in the midst of any war
25/2/84

All things have their beginning,
their allotted space
in the infinite depths
of each one of us,
in them immeasurable
and intimate place
where the visible is forged
and rises up,
and where ideas
are born and live.

This place where
the most sublime and lasting,
the most ephemeral, sinister and execrable
ideas are formed.

Everything comes from inside
with no regard for the surroundings,
without the context conditioning
shouts, voices, exultation,
joy or anxiety.

Each man alone is
responsible for his deeds!

Berlin, 30/10/84

Like the Tiber, shrouded in mist
Everything has been formed
and cannot see
the young, enflamed sap
invigorating the
earth's wasted tree.

The river-beds must fill, run over
and make fertile the parched crust
of the fields and cities,
the thirsting lips
and the numbed skin.

Everything waits, feeling
for a radical change
form the harsh beating sun,
the sterile inertia,
the still water,
feeling for that defiant breeze
to begin blowing
and break in on each one of us;
for imagination
to find new ways
of showing
hidden inspiration;
until the spirit of man
has awoken
travelling
    and covering
        the ground;
for the message of meaning
to reach the farthest corner
and the most distant ear. . .

From this hidden place where I shout
peace not war
I want to see one day soon
that this force is already visible
. . . that the fertile Tiber has emerged!

For Matilde & Juan A. Carrillo
Rome – The Vatican, 21/1/85

Don't interrupt this silence
this voice of the universal
sea
this clamour of stars
that speak meaningful
languages
to the humble,
with your improper,
pretentious
moaning.
Listen
to the eternally new
message
of the wind
and the night!

Salobreña, 22/8/85

Don't come with your palest
lantern
when there is so much brightness
filtering
    from the night
        and from the sea
            almost
                infinite.

Salobreña, 23/8/85

'. . . se me ha muerto
como del rayo. . .'
Miguel Hernández
(Elegía a Ramón Sijé)

Destiny has struck you down
in the fullness
of your flight,
    of your youth,
        of your horizon.

Unbelievable injustice,
dreadful anachronism!
Today in the thorax
of an unknown
    young man
beats your feminine heart
of twenty,
and life filters through
to two unknown people
    thanks
        to your death
            unprepared for,
        premature, mistimed;

We cannot imagine
that your loveliness
can merge with the earth;
we will always be taking you
    from this grave
        where – incomplete –
            you lie,
and we will make you live again
in the boundless space
of memories and dreams!

For María del Carmen
Madrid, 11/5/85

17

Sad the love
that is near,
      touching,
yet separate,
      apart. . .
not knowing
how to be reborn each morning,
not trying
to discover
new ways and horizons
for the flame
not to gutter,
for the undying embers
to be rekindled!

25 December 1985

Love
is travelling together
along the way,
being companions
along the path
whether straight or twisted.
It simply means
being a hand
that lifts up and caresses
being transformed
in a wandering embrace,
a guiding hand,
man-kind,
woman-kind,
human-kind. . .

For Mother Teresa of Calcutta
26/1/86
Durham, U.S.A.

19

From early morning
the past
is worthless.
Everything is born,
everything dawns
and renews itself
at the new light
of day.
We must leave
despite
the pale brightness.
Only the morning
speaks
and the whole world
thinks itself enlightened.
If night were to fall again
love would conquer
only
the shadows
and the glimmering
way
could be traced anew.
Creators
of undiscovered ways:
the boundless future
awaits.
At dawn,
the past exists
yet now is worthless.

For José Vidal-Beneyto
Madrid, 28/3/86

¿Está el mañana escrito?
(leyendo a Don Antonio Machado)

To copy
such a rift,
to narrow
this gap,
to make fertile
this desert
when harsh memory
stalks
our progress,
memory
both lush
yet desolate,
we must go forward
knowing that only the future
has not died.

For Mikhael S. Gorbachev
Madrid, 28/4/86

I am quiet,
a survivor,
flickering
before the dimming light
that foretells
its irrevocable extinction.
Everything is prefaced
with ending
and yet
nothing is in vain
nothing is empty
or without meaning.
May my fervent mind,
my wakeful life
never become numbed,
though I may be wounded,
though vulnerable
and my knowledge minimal!
Obstinately
I will fight on
until the day
I become for ever
rigid and forgotten.
Everyone's marks
remain although
invisible.
Each gleam
remains imperceptible.
The lamp goes out
but lives on undying
the invisible
trace
        of your deeds
        of your words
        of your shouts,
        of your silence.
All of us form the world,
            all of us.
All of us comfort
some weeping
or staunch
some wound.

Salebreña, 4/8/86

Elusive and splendid
like spray
like the wave

gentle or angry.
Why do you disturb me,
why do you oppress me
powerful, sparkling sea,
showing me the levity
or your – of my! –
moments?
Everything is incidental,
everything ends.
why does the mind
        imagine,
    have insight
    on infinity?
How they draw me
    and hurt me
your ephemeral
waves,
your crash
and your wakeless
spray!

Salobreña, 17/8/86

Who swathes you in mist
my sea,
our sea?

Who muddies
your waters and worries
your fish and seaweed?

Who wrongs
this child
playing on the beach?

The air, water and earth
belong to him
and to those yet to be born. . .

Who dares
tarnish
his silver horizons?

For my grandchildren
Salobreña, Summer 1986.

Slacken this sail,
this sail of mine
that can't withstand
        the strong wind.

Day has come.

Day has come
to give this vessel
new spirit
and a new shore.

Slacken the sail.

Day has come.

Salobreña, Summer 1986.

The sea
will still be here
bearing waves
when you and I
are no longer.

Such sadness,
such happiness
to think
that the sea
will still be here
timelessly
bearing waves
when you and I
are no longer!

Salobreña, 6 August 1986

I am so wretched,
sea,
I am so poor,
and you with your wealth
of depth,
of colour
and horizons.

Powerful,
vast sea!

And yet
you cannot withstand my strength:
I look at you,
know you,
love you.

Salobreña, Summer 1986.

Without the measure
of frontiers,
everything goes too far
and oversteps itself.
With neither rules
nor staves
we find no place for us
to hide
our fear
and helplessness.
Bewildered,
we know no limits.
we hurry on
not knowing
        where.

For Jesus Moneo
La Granda, Asturias,
30/8/86

When autumn
shows all colours
          and shades
imaginable
in flowers and leaves
near the intense blue
of Issyk-Kul lake,
reflecting the luminous
                    white
of the surrounding
snowy mountains,
a ray of hope
suddenly appeared
          timidly,
on our weary, doubting
               brows.
A gleam of new light
has given us youthful vigour
and our eyes have caught sight
of an unknown path.
On the shores of Lake Issyk-Kul
our arms opened
          unexpectedly
and our eyes resolutely
          accepted
a compelling challenge of love.
There, in the far-off place
of all colours and shades
I felt and wrote with strength
these simple words of conviction:
the solution lies in seeing together,
talking together, walking hand in hand.

For Ksana, Ela & Marina.
Kirghiz,
Frunze, USSR.
14/10/86

Here I am
in this half-light,
in this ambiguity
both harsh and kind,
though I strive
to break away
and fly free
before
boundless
    night
        restrains
           me. . .

Madrid, 27/11/86

I must heal so many scars
in my wounded body,
so many blows
far deeper than the skin
in this struggle.

I must hurry
and staunch
this bleeding
that swamps
and submerges
before I can
          finally
take flight
          each day!

For Justo Jorge Padrón
Madrid-Moscow
13/2/87

It wants to be a keel
        without a ship.

The body does not know
that the day
        is dying. . .

Don't let it awaken
        and take me over!

Let it fly,
        and dream of being wings,
                without a bird!

Salobreña, August 1987.

I am sorry to leave this void
this vast emptiness,
this senseless shore.

But I am going. . .
and the sea is going with me!

For Andrea
Salobreña, 9 August 1987.

When dawn breaks
colouring the trees of Tais
and the birds take
     their first flight
in Djouj,
Africa unveils
the myriad obscuring
her heart,
her immense diversity. . .

In the proud offices
of the north
they do not know that the dry branches
of the baobab
are full of life
– like the earth –,
that the singers intone
     songs of oblivion,
and that the desert sand
will build the future.

Yamoussoukro, 29 January 1988.

Us-others

In the north
they die of anomie
and boredom,
of society's harshness
and disgust.
They age
from merely looking.
They no longer hope
nor pity.
No-one hounds them
and yet they feel
intimidated.
They die alone
and so pitied!
Gradually
the bleak wind at dusk
takes on the agony
of routine,
of withdrawal. . .
I can understand it all
apart from remaining impassive
when so many voices
clamour for our life!

Dakar, Senegal
January 1988

'C'est la nuit
qu'il est beau
de croire à la lumière'
E. Rostand

Weave and unweave
the strands of your life,
each emotion
and each thought
on this journey
of no return.

Don't lay aside
your courage
so soon,
everything
starts anew
each morning.

Don't despair,
the sun
always
shines through
in the end.

For Jean Millerioux
Paris, 16/2/88

'El desierto
avanza. ¡Ay
de los que
oculten los
desiertos!'
F. Nietzsche

Is immensity with no life
the skin of paradise?

Doubtless it is this
the other ocean
that evokes the infinite.

The dunes,
waves shaped
      by the wind,
like water motionless
as if the sea
had held itself back.

The worth of shade
is only
appreciated in the desert,
which stays
for ever
like love, like fear,
with me.

Chinguitti,
Mauritania
February 1988

Here is the sublime proof:
where I stand the sea begins
and the desert ends
here on the thread
of such vastness!

I must leave
and take refuge in the city
before night falls,
not to feel
    – besides –
the weight of the stars
on my confused brow.

Sand and sea
give the most beautiful sound,
sand and sea
mirror the eternal.

Nouakchott, Mauritania
24 February 1988

I am not going
nor are you staying,
and it's all until next time.

Don't grieve:
tears run dry
but the echo and the current
run deep.

Paris, February 1988.

Algiers 'the white one'
wakes up,
a thousand years old, yet new,
birds in her branches
and diadems of olive trees
on her head.

Tremblings of peace
and of truce
fashion
and groove
the sea and the sand,
multicoloured
border of tiles
scattered on the ground.

Free, emancipated,
beautiful Algiers
appears radiant
in the light
because she knows
how long and black
is the night.

Algiers
11.3.88

We fly propelled
through intense blue
of the sky
through the white,
        white clouds,
over the green savannah
of tumbleweed
and scattered trees.
Africa has all the splendours:
forests, desert, snow,
lakes, sea,
rivers. . .
and the clinging impression
of absence, of emptiness. . .
So many lives and riches
where have they gone?
The Zambezi flows
brimming with life,
determined
to carry
its fate
downstream.

Livingstone, Zambia
20/3/88

How is it possible
for life to continue
when children
tremble with hunger
when all is silent
in the jungle
all except death?

'No news' in the world,
'nothing of interest'
announce the newspapers
of the full-bellied. . .

(From here, routine
is as obvious an accomplice
as a murder weapon)

The chains have already been broken,
black woman dressed in black
wound with a sling
          so wide
the eyes betray
          flashing
while the full lips
repeat the firm resolve
to fight unceasingly
for a dawn
full of light
for your people.

Dark your enlightened
          skin
and dark your scarf

The colour of your mourning
is the most beautiful
I have ever seen!

For Graça Machel
Maputo, Mozambique
26 March 1988

There you remain, fettered,
giving us freedom –
your hands wide open.
Today we want you to know
that each feather
on our wings of liberty
bears the imprint of your prison bars;
that we are determined travellers
along the pathways
your captivity inspires;
that from your prison cell
you free and release
those hearts anchored
in indifference,
and with the strength
of your living example
you break the patterns
of agreements,
of resolutions and consensus
that did not respect with integrity
the dignity of each man,
dignity you strive for and proclaim
with your shackles and chains.

For nelson Mandela, on
his 70th birthday
(imprisoned for the past
26 years – his only crime:
being born black)
May 1988

Here we are, putting our stamp
on print and more print,
visas and more visas,
passed and approved. . .
while the world
passes us by,
slips out of our hands
while children,
    men and women die
without knowing why
        nor for whom.

Zealous civil servants
filling in forms
      forms
        forms
while life passes us by,
while young people yawn
    – with hunger or boredom –
and bureaucrats,
technocrats
keep using papers to fend off
the implacable rebellion
of the spirit.

Lusaka, Zambia
29 March 1988

Although badly wounded
I appear unhurt.

My mind cannot cope with
such oblivion

of my fellow men
alone, isolated,
ignorant,
hungry,
while here we revere
money,
the banker,
the general
       military salute,
       military salute,
       military salute. . .
all in uniform,
all uniform,
       marking time,
       marking time.

From the great windows
they attentively follow
our timid beat,
while the street waits for
the platoon of intellectuals
and the bird of peace
cannot find his nest.

Madrid and Oviedo
21/4/88

And Father Nile
nears the sea.

Slow, solemn,
he arrives at the end
of his journey,
fertile
limit
of the desert.

In the waters
are reflected
the greatest beauties
the human mind
has conceived,
and avid lips
quench their thirst
on the banks.

Father Nile,
weary perhaps by now
does not appear bitter
though
at the climax
of his tremendous run.

Cairo,
27 June 1988

Rising out of the earth,
from stone
– symbol of splendour,
            of strength –
of many-coloured beauty
ravaged by the harsh,
inclement,
adverse weather.
Here, in the heights,
precarity
allows for no weakening
of the creative force
of this people
sculptured in history,
immersed in the future.
The spirit builds
on lamentation
and the alabaster
and multicoloured crystal
create the most rare
harmony,
Sana'a, innermost city,
closed yet open,
ornament
now mine
for ever.

Sana'a, Yemen
30/6/88

What it is
to live in love:
each wrinkle of yours,
              of ours,
draws me more than the smoothness
of other hands
of other arms outstretched
seeking the autumn
of my lips.

In the lines of your skin
our story is there,
each moment
is imprinted,
each smile
and each sorrow.

My wife,
my friend.

Tokyo, 19/9/88

I will raise my voice
each morning,
each evening,
each night.

Non-stop
my cry will resound
in the ears
of the elite
until the whole
world is filled
with love.

While I still live
and still have the power
                of speech
I will shout to the winds
of each new day
that there should be no truce
until every yoke
has been lifted.

For Chinguiz Aitmatov
Paris, 21 September 1988

You looked at me
as I went by.
Flags and sirens
proclaimed my rank.
You, indifferent,
to one side
of the road.
You and me,
both transient passers-by,
both alone
clothed in our own mystery.
How I would have loved
to reach up to you
and tell you
I am fighting
each day
to break the chains
of your monotony!

Beijing, 26 September 1988.

The dream within me
I shall keep
as long as I breathe.

This dream
is my life,
a dream of love
alive at last
in each one of us.

Paris, October 1988

There is so much coldness of love
so much cold
on this bleak horizon
of progress
          of the machine
that we must relentlessly
paint over
with another colour,
with another feverish
          warmth.

Paris, October 1988.

Such silence
and voices
in your waters;
such indecipherable,
accumulated
memory,
yet the perceptible
and almost offensive
impression
that suddenly,
you will recite
all the verses
within you.
The sea, the seas
receive you
River Duero
at the end of your Iberian journey
divided,
united through your fertile
run,
water ribbon
indestructible, permanent
you are born again
in the ocean
to which you belong
for ever.

For Mario Soares
Oporto, 11 November 1988

They filled my hands with flowers
and my neck with garlands.
Oh, no, don't bow down to me.
Your welcome makes me blush
and reminds me
that you have nothing to thank me for!
. . . Later we climb
to the Swayambhnatu Temples
where the mystic
is our equal,
preceded as we are by banners,
trumpets, ringing of bells
and prayers.
You, young lama,
and I
together have felt
the same light and dark.
Beyond,
looms invisible,
yet so certain,
Everest.
In this land high and steep
people are born, survive
and die
unnoticed,
indescribable.
While we go to mass on Sundays
and holy days,
hold raffles and draws
in guise of charity
and regulated everything,
even love. . .
you – and you, young lama –
think we have understood
nothing.
Neither the manager, nor the cross,
nor the message of Buddha, your lord.
When I leave you among the offerings
and lamps of Swayambhu
I know that
we have still not learned
to love.

Katmandu, 17/12/88

The sun's
first light is silver
then purple
before rising
solemn
beyond the mountains.
From lake Tana
the Nile
– The Blue Nile –
begins its long journey.
(Everything is far from here.
Everything except misery,
except the incomparable nobility
of these children
barefoot
hidden away
in this place
of such beauty.
Sculpting in memory
wanting to let nothing
escape me
– although it hurts –
that can be felt:
I watch for each sight,
each smell,
each noise,
so that I forget nothing
of what should be
each day
unforgettable).

Holy land,
tree-like land,
worn, dry,
over.

The water
dried up
long ago.

Desert
covers almost everything,
and there remains only
that which came
out of the sand
never again
to be hidden:
the word.

Doha-Amman
17/2/89

We must build everything
in a place which is
in the middle of nowhere,
near the abyss.
Further off, at the edge
of the rich countries,
the unknown marshes.
(No, not unknown,
the ignored marshes
where our past
flounders
more and more
daily confronted
with the indifferent
and distant
eyes
of the poor
who cannot,
who don't know,
of the wealthy
who don't hear,
who don't wish to know. . .).
To preserve the memory,
the traces of man,
his ways,
to explain
his steps of tomorrow
we must, my children,
            my friends,
            my strangers,
build everything
near the abyss,
in the rugged and unique
space
of our future,
the sole sharable
wealth.

For Javier Pérez de Cuéllar
Los Angeles, 27/2/89

Surrounded
and alone.

My eyes
brim over
bitterness
of acid tears,
sour,
hidden
mixture.

Sorrows
and stinging
cilices
and oblivion.

No-one
remembers
the risk
I have run.

No-one recalls
the enlightened
night
I have lived.

No mark
nor sign
accredit me.

I am surrounded
and alone. . .

Awake,
and I return
to the light
– fainter today –
of each
day.

28/2/89

Canto porque no puedo callar. .
(Argentina tango)

Don't throw away
the poems you wrote
exasperated
in that village
of adobe huts
and mud tracks!
Don't stop saying
they have settled
the debt
by means of teachers
and nurses,
while traffickers
multiply their networks
of profiteering and silence.
Someone will have to be shamed,
someone will have to pay this bill
contracted with the poorest
of the land.
We must hurry:
time goes by,
one day more, one day less
to forge
new bounds
of love and tenderness,
all of us together must do
what only with money
for money alone
would not be done.

For Sister Raquel
March 1989

It was in vain
that dawn
of outlines,
of colours and strokes.

Their shouts subsided
and the bravery
of the proclamation
yesterday inflamed,
today is haggard,
numb.

The square is deserted
when I enter
the streets
of our common,
pallid destiny. . .

Was it in vain?
Perhaps not.
Perhaps that dawn
guides my steps.

3/3/89

Who will heed the voice
of the lonely?
A disregarded cry for help
is the worst
of all laments,
the most painful
of cries.

Abuja, Nigeria
5/4/89

Each morning I will laugh.

I will laugh when the sun rises,
in the evening,
in the gentle night.

I will laugh on a dull
and rainy day,
in the storm,
in thunder and lightening,
I will laugh.

On asphalt,
on the mountain,
in the sea,
I will laugh.

Every day I will laugh
if you regain
your smile.

And never again
will I stop laughing at
a silly thought.

Those black days
have taught me
to laugh,
and not to forget
happiness.

Madrid
8/5/89

Everything is strange
       the largest
       the smallest
       the furthest away
       the nearest
       you
       I.

Everything is still to be learned.

Hesitatingly we begin to advance
to discover,
to know something.

A thread
of light,
the slightest
glimmer
that each person conveys
is a great
glow
in the night falling
immensity
that surrounds us,
that encircles us.

Paris,
17/5/89

*'One must be the first
to receive the other
with a smile'.*
Buddha

Being witness
to so much
and yet
not shouting out
though it all
concerns me.

Where is
freedom?

Where are the prophets?

Hidden,
      silent.

Who should we believe in?

My eyes
and my ears
are filled
with deeds,
events,
weary.

Where can I
sign myself in
for ever?

17/5/89

Time
    passes
and our hands
    remain
        empty.

The minutes
    go by
and nothing comes
    to our waiting.

17/5/89

Today says nothing
of yesterday.
The words lose
their form
and change
with time.
As everything:
words
like water
run
along the narrow
riverbed
of meanings
toward the limitless
sea
of creation
in each one of us,
humble
anchored
in this meagre
flesh,
fading. . .

Paris, 17/5/89

They will bring you
solemnly,
wreaths of flowers
and will burn in your memory
an undying
flame.

But you will have died
you alone,
for a cause
that was
to be lived.

They will place
chrysanthemums and roses
on your grave
while the memory of you
and the reason
why you fell
will
fade away. . .

For unknown soldiers
25/5/89

Again
the bullets of power
silence
young voices
asking for freedom.

Again
the tanks
confront men,
confront shouting,
again
brute force
pushed away the dreams
of so many years. . .

And the light
that had begun
to shine on the horizon
turned into a bloody
storm
into harsh gnashing
turned to damaged clouds
turned to tears
in the great square
of our common future.

3/6/89

They sought to catch me
        in full flight.

    To bring me down
as low as possible today,
to the round
of restrictions
of every day,
of every dawn
and every sunset.

Hidden in the mud
they let fly the arrows.
From reality,
from the night
they sought to catch me
        in full flight.

But their bows are not strong enough
to bring down
ideals,
accustomed, as they are,
to gale-force winds.

Paris, 25/10/89

'¡Que bellos los pasos
del mensajero de la
paz sobre el monte!'
San Francisco de Asís

Does everything depend
on the messenger's
survival?

No.
You must remember that
only
ideas
survive,
not envoys.
Messengers die
a natural death
or are murdered.

It makes no odds:
his message
is everlasting.

Only ideals
allow for passing
from the impossible
to the probable.

November 1989

*'Co-operative neighbourhood
in which frontiers became
bridges'.*
President Von Weizsäcker

Stone after stone
your mighty bulk
will fall.
Stone after stone
the false
despotic
frontier
will yield.
We shall remove
all trace
of your ugliness.
The winter was long
but yet again
the dream of a people
has toppled walls.
Liberty
through a latecomer
always wins in the end.

Paris (Berlin)
20/11/89

'Estoy aquí otra vez
para subrayar con mi sangre
la tragedia del mundo,
el dolor de la tierra,
para gritar con mi carne:
ese dolor es mío también'.
León Felipe
(in 'Español del éxodo
y del llanto')

Tyrant:
you opened fire
on the crowd.
Silence:
children have died,
their temples
and their ears
shattered by shrapnel;
children have been tortured
and beaten.
The soldiers
did not obey
the command to shoot,
to kill their brothers:
bursts of firing
can do nothing
against the rebellion,
weapons always lose
against an embrace.
Sweet-smelling flowers
deck the rifles.
Timișoara:
from now on
we will hold your
bloodied
imprint
in our eyes
and in our minds.
And your dead
will live in each free day
of the liberated people.

Paris, 21/12/89

72

'Cada quien en su mar,
sabiendo que hay un sólo mar'.
Santiago Genovés

The liturgy
keeps us apart
when the spirit
so unites us.

The spirit
not converted
into a rite,
knows and feels
essential things
the essence
of things.

Paris, 16/1/90

Words
– like men –
do not exist
if they are silent.

We know,
and therefore
have no
excuse.

How can we
find sleep,
being accomplices?

Paris, 20 January 1990.

'La partida tenía que ser
triste como toda partida
verdadera; álamos, sauces,
cordillera, todo parecía
decirme no te vayas!'
Nicanor Parra (Chile)

'Stay,
stay here. . .'
friendly voices
from here
have said over again to me.

But I must return
to the heat
of my coldness,
to the wakening
of my people
though knowing
that the night
will be long
and the weather harsh.

Paris, 21/1/90

Light
comes to your face
and colours
it golden
while it lingers.
Twice a year,
punctual watch of the stars
excluding the god of shadow
at your side,
likewise rescued
form the waters.
So early
you overran
all limits
in the colossal
          enormity
of your Pharaonic
sculpture.
But your soul,
however,
as with every
human being,
has at its base
the writing!
Deified in Nubia,
the god-king
also died.
Also died?

Abu Simbel, Upper Nile
Egypt, 11/2/90

The water
took away her school.
Along the lunar, fertile wadi
the rain turned into
a muddy torrent
and Muna's little school
went sailing
along the wide watercourse.
Your black eyes,
little girl with neither books
not pencils,
will travel with me
to wealthy countries:
I will tell them
that Muna's school
was swept away
by the wadi!
Ah! the children
of those countries
don't know
there are schools
that the water takes away.
They don't know there are children,
                              children
              and more children. . .
with neither school nor water!

For Muna
Tarim, Wadi Hadramout
Yemen, 14/2/90

The most ancient
vestige
of urban life,
marvel of symmetry
and nevertheless of beauty,
has been
wounded by the salt
that runs
bitter
along its seams.
Beside it
the great
river
– smoothly
flowing today,
proudly –
destroys
all it touches.
Redeemer
of the waters
keeps,
silent,
arcane mysteries
in its fertile
belly.

Moenjodaro
Pakistan, 11/3/90

Y no entiendo soldadito
a quien te ha puesto en
las manos un fusil y no
una pluma, un fusil y no
otra mano. . .
F. Mayor Menéndez, 1975

Tanks,
tanks,
more and more,
so many, many
tanks.
The officers'
military decorations
gleaming in the sun.
The last
and every single one of them
marches past
– keeping in step, in step –
with the latest
model of machine-guns.
How many desks, classrooms,
books, openings,
could those guns be worth!
(The friendly powers
don't understand
such things. . .
and the nation
must be safeguarded. . .
And the people?
And the peoples?)
'Hear the anthem. . .
            Attention!'
. . . thousands of soldiers file by
and burnished armoured cars
while millions
live bowed down,
on bended knee
they keep imploring
us to have
the courage
to end the farce
and, finally, let them stand.

Wherever, 13/3/90

'La tarde elemental ronda la casa.
La de ayer, la de hoy, la que no pasa'
Jorge Luis Borges in
'La tarde', of 'Los conjurados'.

I took a break
to be with myself
because I am without you.

They do not know
the constant message
            of the memory
    of your deep eyes;
not the voice of your absent lips,
when speech
is not possible
nor necessary
– beautiful language
of silence! –
to be lived. . .

And I want to be alone
because I am without you
to be with you.

Solitude is sweet, my love,
if it is wished!

Quebec
3/4/90

'Tota la vida
treballàvem sense esma,
no ha estat possible.
Ara les hores tornen
i ens troben fets i dòcils'.
Jesús Massip, in the
'Llibre d'hores'.

Are you complaining
about the strong surge of feeling?
For that we want
the bravery
of those who do not accept
merely
the visible.

Calm is submission,
depression,
death.

Life
is in the whirl
where the wind lashes
and each cell shakes
and believes
in the impossible.

Only rebels
are beacons
for the change
that the human condition
demands.

Ottawa, Canada
5/4/90

In the ashes
embers,
fire,
and the iron
at last red hot,
yet there's no-one
now,
to forge it.
(The forge,
with such a blacksmith
might be empty.)
I do not fit in
yet measured words
in my mouth form
the opposite remark,
cautiousness
not to break
the established rules;
to follow
the same tedious course
that steers toward
nowhere;
to repeat the same
well-established round;
to be ever gently flowing
never rushing
into a great river. . .
Rhetoric,
heavy emptiness
fills it all
while outside
it is cold
and night is falling.

London 10/4/90

'*No he de callar*. . .'
Góngora

Hunger, hunger,
weapons, weapons, weapons. . .

I plan to rise up
and rebel
and shout out
everywhere
I want to go
to no more wars.

I am not crying.
But my lips
proclaim
with strength
that docility
has ended.

Paris
8/5/90

Today,
is grey.

Grey is the colour
of everything
this morning: the mist
                    the grass
                    the city
                    the sky
                    the hill
                    the sea. . .

All is grey.
The whole horizon,
also grey.

All that can be
                    seen
                    and thought, grey. . .

Only love
could, yet,
brighten
the day.

30/5/90

. . . '(j'écris) pour que le
roi y prenne un conseil,
qu'il connaisse dorénavant
la puissance de la parole' . . .
Ferdowsi
(le Livre des Rois, 990)

Let us raise our voice,
our strength.

We come with neither arms
nor money.

They will try to silence us
by force
with gags
or gifts
and honours.

But each time
there will be more and more
of us speaking
                out, shouting out!
openly,
multilingual,
meaningful,
new verses.

Our song will soar
and reach the ears
of the most powerful.

And in the end it will be the word
that will guide the steps
of man.

For Leopold Sédar Senghor
Salobreña – Tangiers
13/8/90

The bora-bora
drank the remaining
water.
And the marshlands
within a few days
held no trace
of the pathways
so well marked out!
The Indian looked
at the 'experts'
while thinking:
how little they know
of the living forest!

1/9/90

There was no money
for the starving
nor for the uninformed.
But now, suddenly,
they have opened up
the coffers of war
and thousands of millions
stream to the front!
There was no money
for peace,
for the fight against drugs,
for the environment.
God, what blindness!
There was no money for peace,
but there is for war.

Paris, 15/9/90

The dead are not dead,
They are here
in this copper
old and battered,
in this vase,
in these outlines. . .
In these ruins
the creative force
remains intact
sole right
of mankind.
All are living
nameless
or known
in each moment
of the legacy
of history.
The dead have not died
completely.
They all lie in the shadow
of our fragile
and docile
everyday life
of our duty,
of our potential
present.

Saint Malo
8/10/90

señalaba su frente con el dedo
indice, en Palafrugell, 1976.

Each day
we are reminded
by physiology
that all of us in the end
are equal,
there are no categories
for mother earth,
everything returns to her
as deposits and ashes
only the human mind
flies over matter
and dwells
in the infinite space
it creates.
Making possible
this miracle
in each woman and each man
is of all our
duties
the one most kinding.

Brussels, 18/11/90